Gatsby Songs

From the Opera THE GREAT GATSBY
(voice and piano)

Music by John Harbison
Lyrics by Murray Horwitz

AMP 8161

First Printing: December 1999

ISBN 0-634-01080-8

Associated Music Publishers, Inc.

DISTRIBUTED BY

HAL•LEONARD®
CORPORATION
7777 W. BLUEMOUND RD. P.O. BOX 13819 MILWAUKEE, WI 53213

PREFACE

In the opera THE GREAT GATSBY, five songs are sung in the course of small or large gatherings, either over the radio or live by a Band Vocalist. These songs, with lyrics by Murray Horwitz, bear a resemblance to popular songs from the 1920s, but also share musical elements with the score as a whole. A number of other songs appear in the opera as instrumentals only. After the completion of the opera, Murray Horwitz wrote lyrics for these as well, completing the present collection, which reorders and rearranges the songs, making them presentable separately or as a sequence.

—JOHN HARBISON

THE GREAT GATSBY

Music and libretto by John Harbison
after the novel by F. Scott Fitzgerald
with popular song lyrics by Murray Horwitz

Commissioned by the Metropolitan Opera to commemorate
the 25th anniversary of the debut of James Levine

BY THE SHORE

Murray Horwitz

John Harbison

3

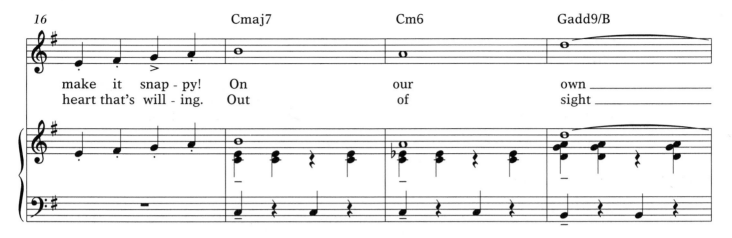

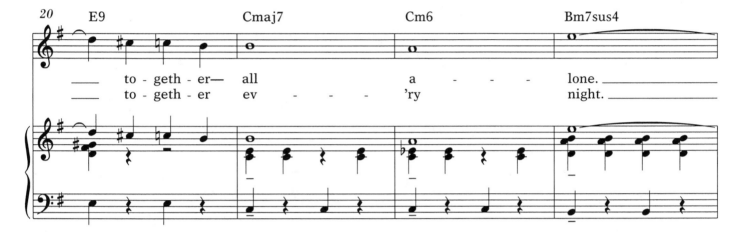

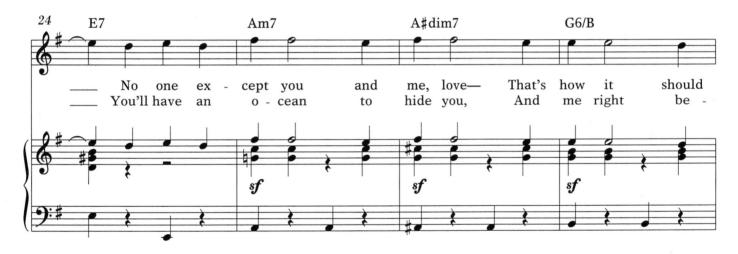

KIND OF IN LOVE

Murray Horwitz

John Harbison

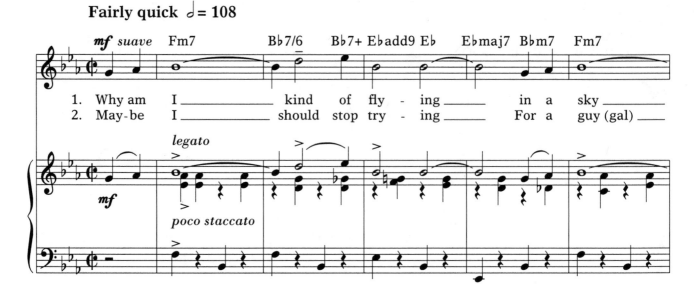

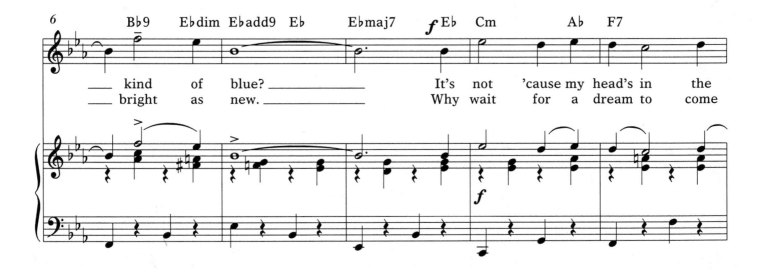

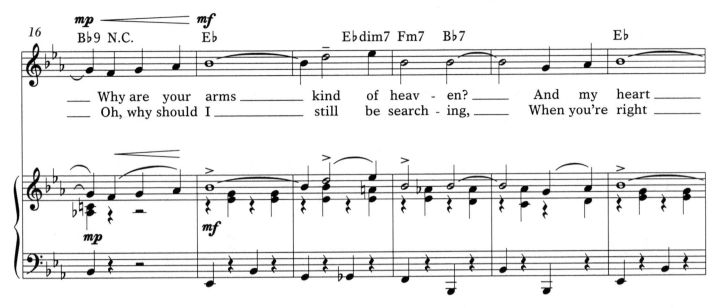

6

FUNNY NEW FEELING

Murray Horwitz

John Harbison

A SATURDAY NIGHT TO-DO

Murray Horwitz

John Harbison

I'M LEAVIN' IT ALL TO YOU

Murray Horwitz

(alternate lyric to "A Saturday Night To-Do")

John Harbison

I COULD END UP LOVING YOU TONIGHT

Murray Horwitz

John Harbison

DREAMING OF YOU

Murray Horwitz

John Harbison

16

* When singing solo, sing the descant for the next 8 measures.

* When singing solo, return to lower staff.

BLOWING A BUNDLE ON YOU

Murray Horwitz

John Harbison

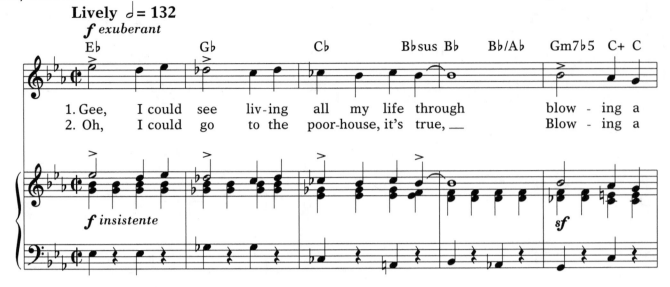

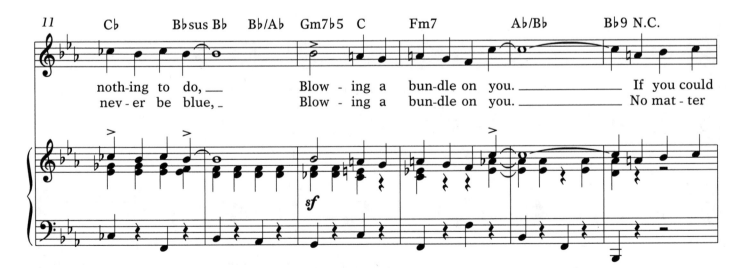

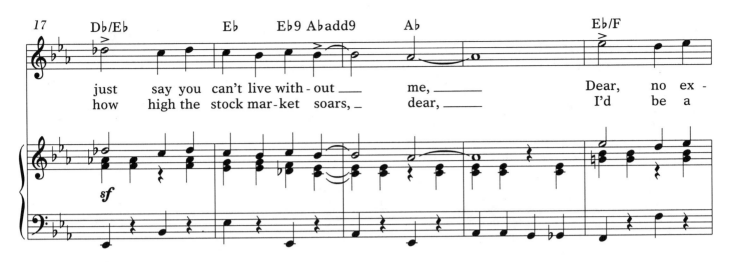

I CAN'T BELIEVE IT

Murray Horwitz

John Harbison

Comfortably, easy ♩ = 80

mp warmly

1. I can't be - lieve it. Life seems to be fine. _____ I can't be -
2. I can't be - lieve it. How sil - ly I feel! _____ I can't be -

lieve it. Love seems to be mine. _____ When bore-dom drowned me,
lieve it. How real - ly i - deal _____ your kind of style is,

You came and found me. Oh, what a hand-some sur - prise! _____
Your kind of smile is. I missed you more than I knew. _____

REMEMBER THE OLD DAYS

Murray Horwitz

John Harbison

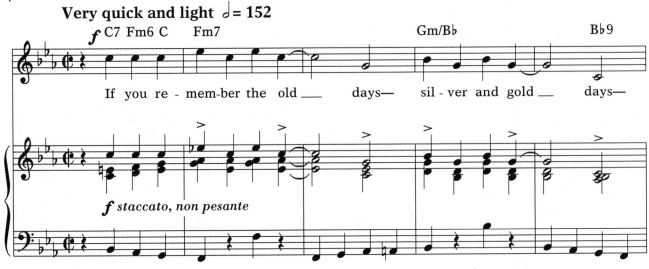

Very quick and light ♩ = 152

If you re-mem-ber the old ___ days— sil-ver and gold ___ days—

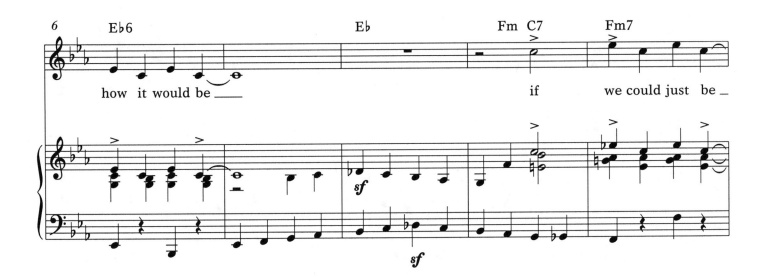

how it would be ___ if we could just be ___

___ there, just you and me ___ there, think what we'd see: ___

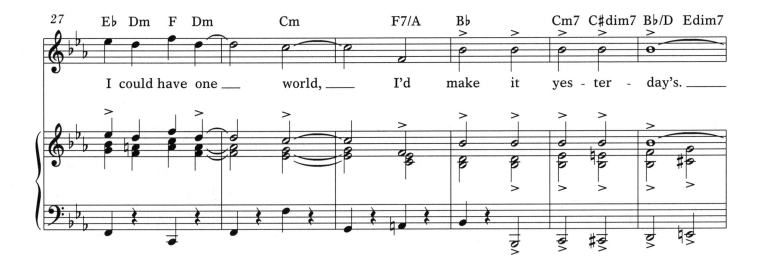

_Seems noth-ing can last ___ now. Think of the past ___ now—_

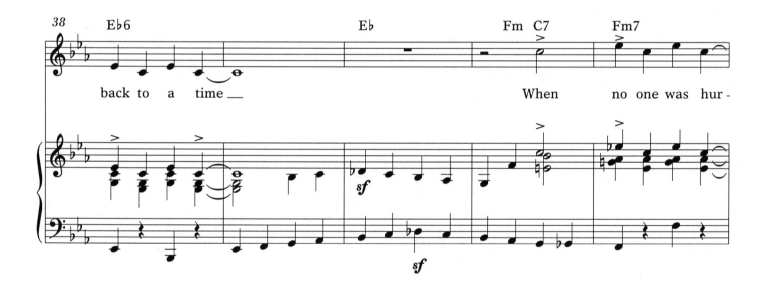

_back to a time ___ When no one was hur-_

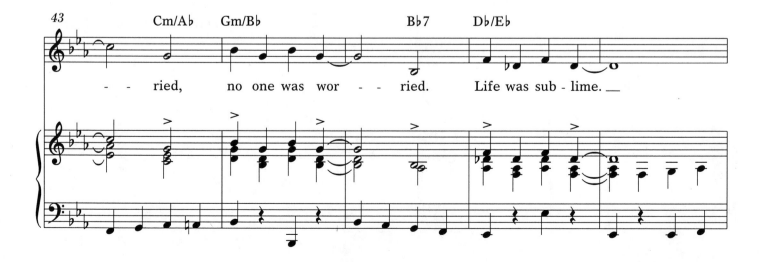

_- - ried, no one was wor - - ried. Life was sub - lime. ____

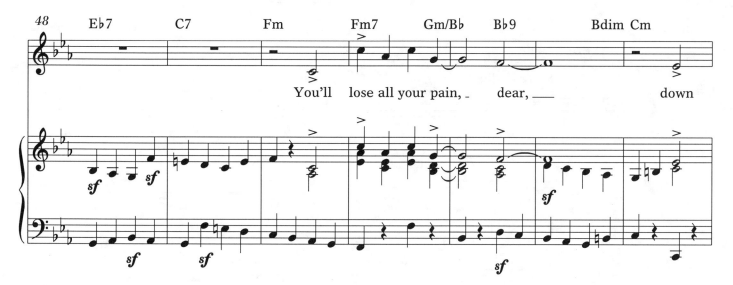

You'll lose all your pain, dear, down

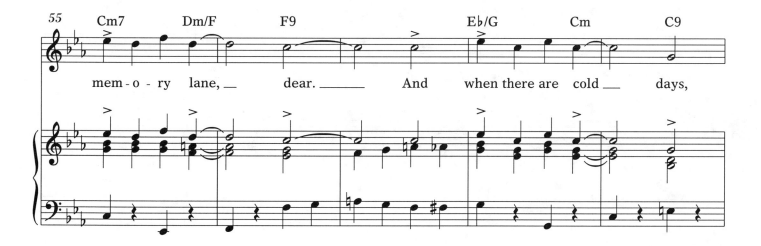

mem-o-ry lane, dear. And when there are cold days,

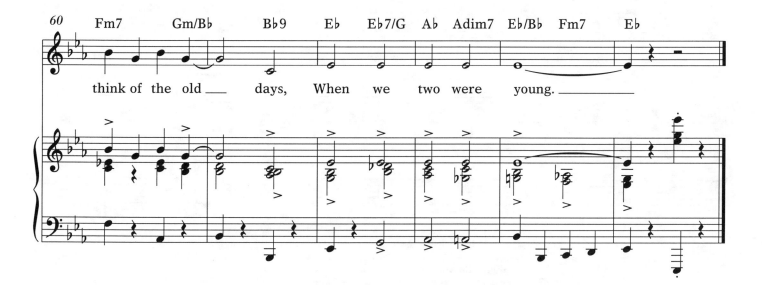

think of the old days, When we two were young.

I'M DOIN' FINE

Murray Horwitz

John Harbison

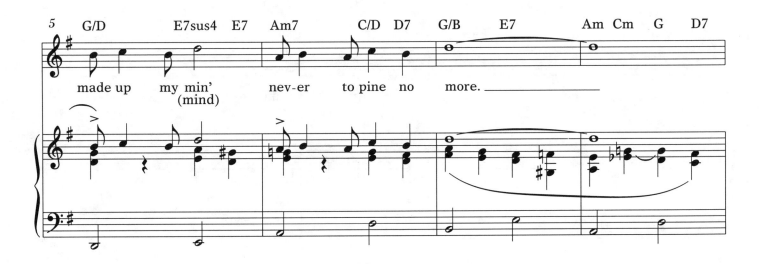

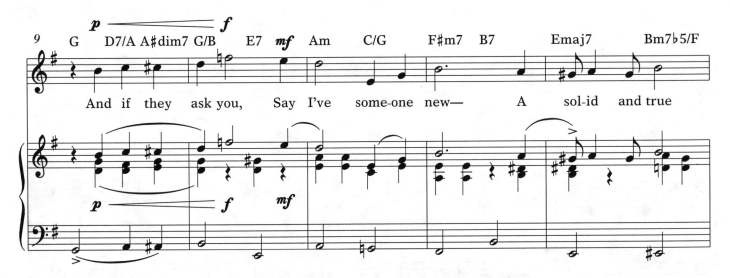

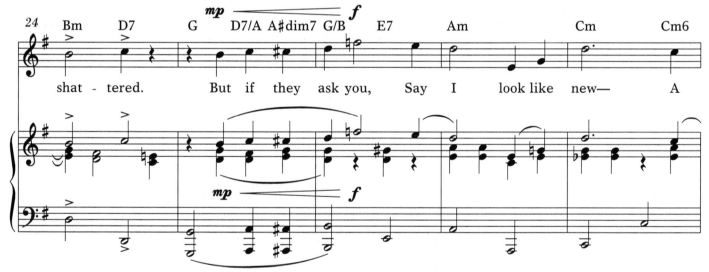

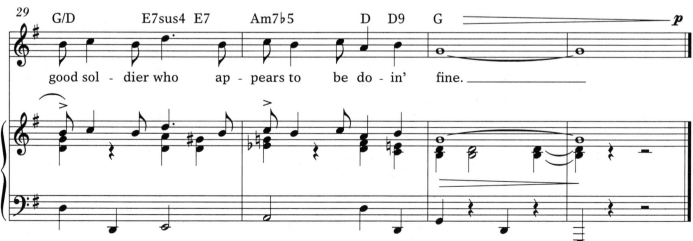

COOL

Murray Horwitz

John Harbison

Easy middle tempo ♩= 88

Cool— like the sum-mer-y o - cean breeze.

Cool— like the ear - li - est morn - ing dew. When my

heart with fi - er - y flame is burn - ing, then I run to quench my de -

WHO CAN SAY?

Murray Horwitz

John Harbison

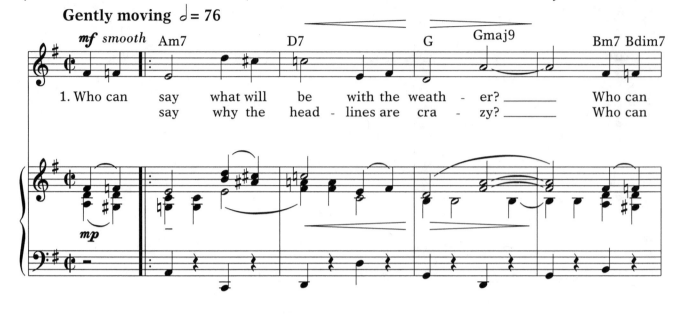

1. Who can say what will be with the weath - er? _____ Who can
say why the head - lines are cra - zy? _____ Who can

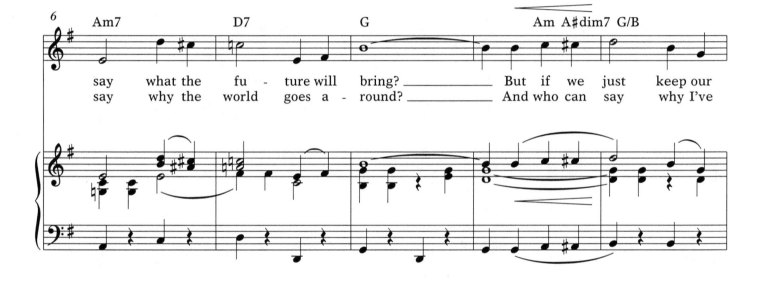

say what the fu - ture will bring? _____ But if we just keep our
say why the world goes a - round? _____ And who can say why I've

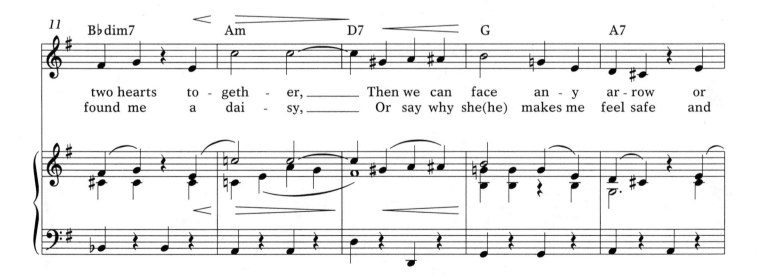

two hearts to - geth - er, _____ Then we can face an - y ar - row or
found me a dai - sy, _____ Or say why she(he) makes me feel safe and

STRANGE

Murray Horwitz

John Harbison

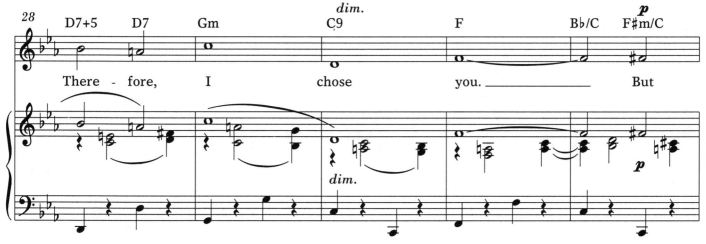

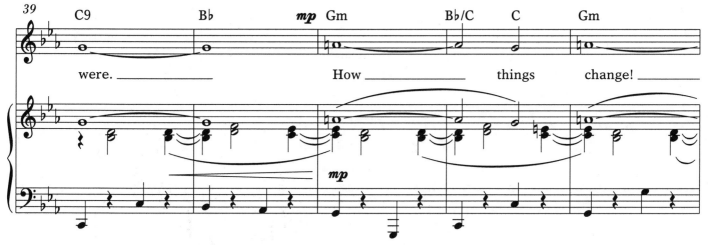